SUPERSAW

FL STUDIO

How to Make a Fat Supersaw Lead in FL Studio for EDM Production

The 3xOsc Supersaw Synth Sound Design Template for Beginners

By Cep from Screech House

ISBN-13: 978-1697940992

ISBN-10: 1697940994

PREFACE

In this unique instruction guide, you will get an ultimate template to design your own professional detuned supersaw lead in FL Studio. With five easy-to-take steps, you will instantly unlock the hidden power of FL Studio's stock synthesizer "3x Osc". Thereby, this is all you have to do:

1. Start with a detuned saw by using the 3xOsc in FL Studio.

2. Give it a natural shape by taking advantage of a volume envelope.

3. Unlock its superpowers by learning how to use fat mode in FL Studio.

4. Quickly fine-tune your supersaw on the FL Studio Channel Rack.

5. Finally, reach that sought-after professional quality by using the Mixer in FL Studio.

So, if you're currently unhappy with how your songs sound or if you're learning how to make EDM music, this is your chance to benefit from this exclusive material.

What can you expect?

As an experienced EDM producer with an influential YouTube channel (https://youtube.com/screechhouse) and author portfolio (https://screechhouse.com/books), I still don't want anyone to blindly believe anything I say. Everyone can talk, therefore it's important to back it up. That's why; let me demonstrate the exact results you are going to achieve today. Just visit the link below to watch a short demo video on my channel.

https://youtu.be/2j-JTzY2Jhg

Why should you know how to make a supersaw lead?

For decades, there has never been a sound so absurdly dominant, that you just have to know its mighty recipe. Yes, we're talking about the holy supersaw.

A supersaw is a type of lead commonly used in EDM genres to make pleasant chord synths and sharp melodies. Therefore, it forms the essential foundation of your sound design and song building. By simply knowing how to make a supersaw lead, you take a giant leap forward in becoming a successful EDM producer.

What is so super about this lead?

First featured on the Roland JP-8000 synthesizer, the name "supersaw" is based upon the actual design of this type of lead. You see, a supersaw simply consists of multiple detuned saw waves forming a whole. Thus, these saw waves playing together create a super massive saw type of sound. Super indeed.

To witness such a sound, just pay attention to the lead melodies or chords in many popular EDM songs. Once you realize its frequent appearance, you will directly understand the importance of having these supersaw-making skills yourself. In conclusion: no supersaw is no EDM track. Basically.

How to make a professional supersaw lead?

However, making such a lead sound professional can be extremely difficult and seemingly impossible. How the heck do the pros get these loud, clean and big supersaws in their songs? And how on earth can you get the exact same results? Clearly, they know some EDM production secrets that you don't.

But what most people don't realize is that, if you know the right strategies, making a fat supersaw synth is easier than riding a bike. In fact, with only one FL Studio synthesizer and a few basic tweaks, you too can get the same remarkable results.

How do YOU create a supersaw?

That's why, to help you make an excellent specimen, I've created this step-by-step instruction guide for you. By simply following it, you will have an exceptional formula that serves as a unique shortcut template.

But before you begin, please watch out that you don't take all steps too literal, as there are many ways of doing things. Always strive to understand what you're doing, instead of blindly following what to do.

Nevertheless, using this instruction guide will be a valuable onramp to kick-start your own high-quality sound design. At the end, you will know exactly how to make a powerful supersaw lead in FL Studio rapidly.

Be prepared

Now before you begin, it's essential that you have FL Studio installed on your computer. FL Studio is the D.A.W. (Digital Audio Workstation) we are going to use to design a stunning supersaw lead. Therefore, make sure you can access this application before reading any further.

Once FL Studio is working and you continue with this guide, you will come across many different settings. These settings have specific meanings and values. To find those meanings and values in FL Studio, just look in the field right underneath the menu. This field is called the "Hint panel". The Hint panel will show the meaning of a certain function when you hoover over it with your mouse. Similarly, once you actually click and move a particular knob, the corresponding value will appear there too. So, keep your eyes on the Hint panel while following all the instructions.

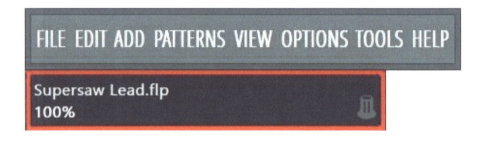

If everything is crystal clear, then let's dive in immediately.

CONTENTS

STEP 1:

HOW TO USE THE 3X OSC IN FL STUDIO

FL Studio contains many different stock plugins that are included in the application, like synthesizers, generators and effects. By using FL Studio stock plugins, you don't need to purchase (expensive) third-party software. Therefore, let's make a fine supersaw lead with FL Studio's classic stock synthesizer: 3x Osc.

The 3x Osc is a basic lightweight plugin capable of producing impressive sounds. That is, if you know how to use it correctly, which most people do not. However, at the end of this guide, you may be one of the few who knows its hidden powers.

Now, to initiate the sound design process, you usually have to start on the oscillators section. On the oscillators section, you can actually generate a soundwave that serves as your starting point. Later, you can tweak it and shape it to change its characteristics. But let's not get ahead of ourselves. Below are the guidelines you can follow to start with your supersaw lead.

1. First, be sure to open FL Studio and start with a new/clean project. If you don't know how to start with a clean project, use one of the built-in templates. Go to "File" in the FL Studio menu, select "New from template", then "Minimal" and click "Empty". Your FL Studio project is now completely empty.

2. Then, click "Add" in the FL Studio menu and select the "3x Osc". The 3x Osc will appear and included as a channel to the Channel Rack.

3. On the 3x Osc, go to oscillator 1 and only do the following:

   ➢ Set the waveform to a saw "Shape" by selecting the corresponding icon. This will give the lead the correct starting sound. After all, we're making a superSAW.

   ➢ Set the "Detune" slider around +24 to +32 by moving it up a bit. This will create a slight pitch difference between the oscillator's signals. As a reminder: you can find the corresponding values in the Hint panel underneath the FL Studio menu.

   ➢ Keep the "Coarse" knob at 24 and the remaining settings default. The Coarse setting dictates the fundamental key/pitch of the oscillator. For now, leave it be.

4. Similarly, go to oscillator 2 and do the following:

   ➢ Set the waveform to a saw "Shape" by selecting the corresponding icon.

   ➢ This time set the "Detune" slider around -24 to -32 by moving it down a bit. This will give oscillator 2 a slightly lower-pitched detune than oscillator 1.

➢ Keep the "Coarse" knob at 12 and the remaining settings default. This results in a one octave difference with oscillator 1.

5. Unlike the other oscillators, go to oscillator 3 and set the "Mix level" knob to 0%. In other words, turn it completely down/off. Oscillator 3 will thereby be deactivated and not be used for this template. This simply leaves two active oscillators playing detuned saw waves.

6. Lastly, at the bottom of the 3x Osc, set the "Phase rand" (phase randomness) to 100% by completely opening the knob. This will give each saw wave a random starting position in their oscillation.

If you're new to FL Studio and these steps and terms sound confusing to you, read the FL Studio Beginner's Guide first. The FL Studio Beginner's Guide explains all the vital FL Studio functions to help you make songs as fast as possible. Start now by visiting this link:

https://screechhouse.com/books/fl-studio-beginners-guide

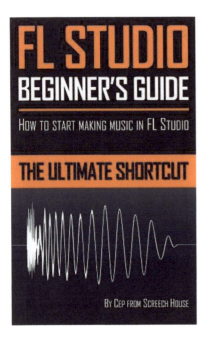

If you're not having any troubles following these instructions, you're ready for step 2. As for now, you have accomplished the first bit of sound design. In the next step, you can determine the volume movement of your lead with an envelope.

STEP 2:

HOW TO USE AN ENVELOPE IN FL STUDIO

After the first bit of sound design on the oscillators' area, it's time to determine the exact movement of the lead. The movement dictates when what happens and for how long. This is where the envelope section comes in. An envelope is a function designed to create certain types of movements with your sound.

For the supersaw lead, you don't necessarily have to create any type of movement. However, you may want to change the volume shape a little bit to get a slightly more natural sound. Therefore, let's use the volume (amplitude) envelope to do exactly that. Simply follow the instructions below.

1. At the top of the 3x Osc wrapper (outer visible layer/edge), click the "Detailed settings" option in the form of a gear icon. This should bring up an extra bar of options.

2. In this freshly brought-up "Detailed settings" bar, click the "Envelope / instrument settings" tab. You can recognize it by its graph-like icon.

3. Underneath the "Envelope / instrument settings" tab, select the "Volume" tab. This will show the volume envelope settings.

4. In the volume envelope area, simply do the following:

    ➢ Fully close the "Delay" knob.

    ➢ Fully close the "Att" (attack) knob. Closing the delay and attack allows the sound to start immediately at maximum volume.

    ➢ Fully open the "Hold" knob.

    ➢ Fully close the "Dec" (decay) knob. Opening the hold and closing the decay allows the sound to stay at maximum volume as long as a note is being played.

    ➢ Fully close the "Sus" (sustain) knob.

    ➢ Open the "Rel" (release) knob a little bit with a short to medium amount. Alternatively, right-click on the "Rel" knob, select "Set" and click "1 step" or "2 steps". This will give your sound a little bit of a natural fade out at the moment a note ends. Of course, you can give your lead a shorter or longer release as you desire. Thereby, the longer the release, the longer the fade-out sound.

That was a piece of cake. Sometimes, a few minor tweaks are needed to finetune a sound based on personal taste. Therefore, you must know the relevant options. But let's do something major this time and make the supersaw ultra **fat** in step 3.

STEP 3:

HOW TO USE FAT MODE IN FL STUDIO

As for now, the lead is still a bit weak and monotone. Therefore, you can use the fat mode section to change that. The fat mode section has the option to produce multiple echoes (voices) of your sound. By playing multiple voices together, you will get a much fuller sound.

In order to get a fuller, smoother and more detuned supersaw lead, you will have to use specific settings on the fat mode section to your advantage. Mind you, this is one of the 3x Osc's secrets most producers don't know about. Yet, after applying the instructions below, you're one of the few who knows exactly what to do.

1. Go to the "Detailed settings" bar on the 3x Osc and click the "Miscellaneous functions" tab in the form of a wrench icon.

2. Between the several miscellaneous functions, find the "Echo delay / fat mode" area and apply the following settings:

   ➢ Fully open the "Feed" knob to 200%. This will produce a completely emerged fat signal with all the voices.

➢ Move the "Pitch" knob very slightly to the right or left and give it a value around +6 to +12 cents. This will give each voice a slightly different pitch. To get these very small amounts, hold the "Ctrl" key on your keyboard while turning the knob with your mouse. While you do that, keep looking at the Hint panel to find the right value.

➢ Fully close the "Time" knob to 0:00. This will layer all voices on top of each other at the exact starting point of the sound.

➢ Set the "Echoes" somewhere around 6 to 8. This will produce multiple additional voices of your sound. You could also go for a higher or lower value, whereas the more echoes the fatter the sound.

➢ Lastly, don't forget to enable fat mode by clicking the "Fat mode" checkbox. This activates the function.

With these instructions being applied, you have transformed your lead from an inconspicuous softy into an undeniable badass. Although the sound is impressive already, you're not done yet. You first need to prepare the supersaw for the ultimate climax by using the Channel Rack in step 4.

STEP 4:

How to use the channel rack in FL Studio

Once you've changed the monotone sound into a fat one, it's time to get some audio feedback. Moreover, you may also want to recover some lost volume and set the lead up for receiving essential effects. Fortunately, all these objectives can be accomplished via the Channel Rack in FL Studio. The Channel Rack is the collector and organizer of instruments called channels. Thereby, it allows for a couple of options you need to use to get the jobs done.

Using the Channel Rack is about the FL Studio workflow and has little to do with the 3x Osc itself. Yet, since this is an FL Studio instruction guide, it's crucial to follow the instructions below to set the supersaw lead up for greatness.

1. At this point, close the 3x Osc and go to the Channel Rack. If the Channel Rack doesn't show, click "View" in the FL Studio menu and select "Channel Rack".

2. On the Channel Rack, find the "3x Osc" channel which on default has the name "3x Osc" written into it. Now, in front of the 3x Osc channel there's a small volume knob called "Channel volume". When you've

found it, fully open it to a level of 100%. This will bring back some lost volume as a result of using the fat mode function.

3. Also, directly in front of the 3x Osc channel, click, hold and drag the "Target mixer track" box and set it to 1. This will route your lead to the Mixer, specifically to Insert Track 1. It will be used at step 5 of this guide.

4. Next, right-click onto the 3x Osc channel and click "Rename, color and icon..." A small editable field will appear.

5. In this field, type in "Supersaw Lead" and press Enter. The name "3x Osc" is now replaced with the text "Supersaw Lead". Renaming your channels like this will help you organize your sounds and instruments, especially useful for bigger projects.

6. Again, right-click onto the 3x Osc channel, but now click "Piano Roll". This will bring up the FL Studio Piano Roll.

7. On the Piano Roll, draw some notes with a length of around 2 steps (half a beat). Preferably, include some chords. Chords are notes part of a musical scale being played simultaneously. For example, click in the Piano Roll to draw a note on C6. Directly underneath, click again to draw a new note on A6. This way, also draw one on E5, A3 and A2, all playing at the same time. This will produce a fat chord. Of course, feel free to experiment and make a short melody, rhythm and/or chord progression. But don't overthink it. As long as there's some musical content on the Piano Roll, you're good for now.

8. When you have some musical content on the Piano Roll, go to the "Transport panel" (playback bar) near the FL Studio menu. On the Transport panel, select "Pat" (pattern) and click the "Play" button. This allows you to listen to your freshly designed sound and melody.

If you want to stop it, simply press the "Stop" button. This way, using the playback function regularly will give you important feedback about the current state of your sound. Thereby, listen and learn what you still would like to modify to furtherly improve your lead.

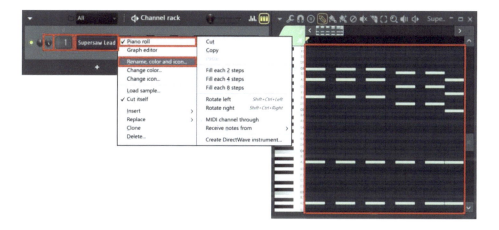

Now, if you're not a gifted musical wonder, there's no need to panic. You too can easily attain powerful melody-making skills, even without knowing music theory. Simply begin with The Ultimate Melody Guide. In this well-received guide, you will discover exactly how to use scales, how to make chords and how to make awesome melodies quickly. Start now by visiting this link:

https://screechhouse.com/books/the-ultimate-melody-guide

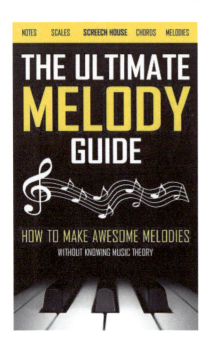

However, if your musicality is already up to par, all props to you. You're now ready for the final step to really bring your supersaw to life. Thereby, you will have to take advantage of the Mixer and implementing the right effects.

STEP 5:

HOW TO USE THE MIXER IN FL STUDIO

Finally, to make your supersaw lead really come to live, you will have to apply some effects. Effects, also called FX, are plugins or functions that can process a sound for a specific purpose. For example, you can add space to your sound with a reverb or you can change its frequency content with an equalizer.

However, to apply effects, you will have to use the Mixer in FL Studio. The Mixer's purpose is to mix and modify the output signals of all the instruments send to it. Thereby, it allows for a variety of different effects to shape a sound in any way imaginable.

As for the supersaw lead, a few Mixer effects are quite crucial to get the desired outcome. Although you can benefit from many more, for the purpose of this guide you only need to add a reverb and equalizer. These will make your lead bigger, sharper, cleaner and more spacy. Find out how via the instructions below.

1. If you haven't yet, close the Piano Roll and open the Mixer by clicking "view" in the FL Studio menu and select "Mixer". This will bring up the Mixer.

2. On the Mixer, click on the "Insert 1" track. This ensures you will be working on the correct Mixer track as the 3x Osc has been routed to it in step 4 of this guide. Needless to say, but if you have routed the 3x Osc to a different Mixer track, you must select that one.

3. Then, click on one of the empty slots (e.g. "Slot 1") and select "Fruity Reeverb 2". The Fruity Reeverb 2 plugin will now appear. The reverb will be used to give the lead a sense of space, fullness and allows it to melt effortlessly in a mix.

4. On the Fruity Reeverb 2, apply the settings below. Mind you, there's a lot of variety possible, so feel free to experiment with different values based on personal taste.

   ➢ Open the "Delay" knob to around 100 to 125 ms. This delays the start of the reverb a little bit which can help prevent the sound to drown too much into it.

   ➢ Open the "Dec" (decay) knob to around 3.0 to 4.0 seconds. This determines the duration of the reverb, whereby a relative long reverb sounds a bit bigger.

   ➢ Open the "Size" (room size) knob to around 80 to 100. A bigger room typically sounds grander.

   ➢ Open the "Mod" (modulation) knob to a depth around 20 to 50. This will vibrate the reverb a little bit to stay in touch with the detuned nature of a supersaw lead.

   ➢ Open the L.cut (low cut) knob to around 250 to 350 Hz (Hertz). This will remove the muddy lower frequencies from the reverb which helps with your mix.

   ➢ Open the "Wet" slider to around 90 to 100%. The wetness determines the amount of reverb being applied. Usually, a supersaw lead fares very well with a good amount of reverb.

5. Once you roughly replicated these settings, close the Fruity Reeverb 2 and click onto a new empty slot on the Mixer (e.g. "Slot 2"). There, find the "Fruity Parametric EQ 2" and click it. The Fruity Parametric EQ 2 will now appear.

6. On the Fruity Parametric EQ 2, only apply the following settings:

   ➢ Go to the last band on the equalizer, which is by default set to a "High shelf" type. Click the circle/dot and move up the "Band 7 level" slider to around 6 to 10 dB (decibels).

   ➢ Then, set the "Band 7 freq" (frequency) knob to around 3500 to 8000 Hz. If you can't find the band frequency, look at the bottom-right of the Fruity Parametric EQ 2 for the parameters. Applying the band level and frequency like this, will add some higher frequencies for freshness and clarity.

   ➢ Next, enlarge the bandwidth to around 75 to 100% by opening the "Band 7 width" knob at the bottom-right of the Fruity Parametric EQ 2. This will introduce the higher frequencies in a more gradual manner.

   ➢ Optionally, use the first band to make a high cut. Therefore, change the "Band 1 type" to "High pass". If you can't find the band type, look at the top-right of the Fruity Parametric EQ 2 in the form of a small graph-like icon. Once you've found it, click, hold and drag it to change the band's shape to a high pass.

➢ Furthermore, move the "Band 1 freq" to around 90 to 180 Hz. Again, located at the bottom-right area of the Fruity Parametric EQ 2. Using it like this will remove some of the lower frequencies to prevent muddiness and rumble in your mix.

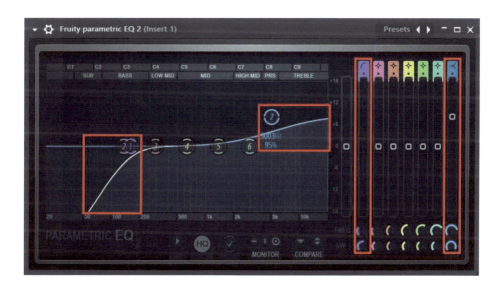

7. As desired, use another free slot on the Mixer to add the Fruity Waveshaper or Fruity Compressor. A waveshaper or compressor can saturate the sound and limit the signal to allow for maximum loudness and power. However, this is not a must and purely dependent on your mix and preferred outcome. Thus, I highly encourage you to experiment, but it falls beyond the scope of this focused guide.

8. Finally, close all the effects and listen to your new impressive supersaw lead by hitting the "Play" button in FL Studio.

There you have it, an easy-to-make fat detuned supersaw lead in FL Studio. Again, these instructions only serve as an example for giving you a great starting point. They form an effective template that you can easily modify and extend onto. So, don't feel like you "have to" do it this way. Feel free to tweak the settings, play around and experiment. For example, you could modify the synthesizer, insert a delay effect or add a chorus. Simply base everything on your own taste and desired outcome.

YOUR NEXT STEP:

SET YOURSELF UP FOR SUCCESS

Clearly, there's more to high-quality sound design (and mixing) than just following some instructions. Nevertheless, this gets you started quickly and effectively. Besides, you just discovered some of the secret strategies I personally use for professional sound design. If that doesn't give an ultimate shortcut, I don't know what does.

Now, to create that important supersaw sound, you've just gone through many different synthesizer settings. Yet, have you already figured out what they do, what they mean and why you should use them? You see, without the vital understanding of all these knobs, you simply have no idea what you're doing. Therefore, if you want to avoid failure and make impressive music effectively, you will have to learn how to work with synthesizers as soon as possible.

That's why, to help you achieve success, I decided to write the entire Sound Design for Beginners guide. This much-needed book explores all the essential basics of sound design and synthesis in full detail. By having this powerful knowledge, you will understand exactly what each setting on a synthesizer does, what it means and why or when you should use it. So, if you want to benefit from this must-know material, start now by visiting the link below.

https://screechhouse.com/books/sound-design-for-beginners

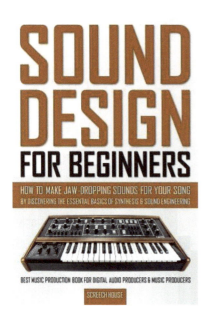

Mind you, it's only temporarily available for a lucrative price.

I'd love to meet you again in my other books, but if you want to learn everything by yourself that's awesome too. Yet, if one day you may need some extra help, just know that my work is available for you. Whether you're looking for a detailed guide, a tutorial video or a quick reply on your comment, just visit me on YouTube (https://youtube.com/screechhouse), Amazon (https://amazon.com/author/screechhouse) or my website (https://screechhouse.com). Or rather, feel free to go ahead and drop by right now.

Talk to you soon.

- Cep

(Music producer, author & CEO of *Screech House*)

GET YOUR FREE SAMPLE PACK

Exclusively for *Screech House* readers and viewers, download a FREE hardstyle sample pack including many high-quality EDM samples. Visit the link below to start your download now.

https://screechhouse.com/free-hardstyle-sample-pack

www.ingramcontent.com/pod-product-compliance
Lightning Source LLC
Chambersburg PA
CBHW041153050326
40690CB00001B/464